Where Will I Spend Eternity?

I0155560

BISHOP R. L. WASHINGTON
MINISTRIES

Imparting the Word to Impact the World

Where Will I Spend Eternity?

A Companion Guide to the Book of REVELATION

by

Bishop R.L. Washington Sr.

Where Will I Spend Eternity?
Copyright © 2024—Rodrick L. Washington Sr.
ALL RIGHTS RESERVED

All Scripture references are from the *Holy Bible, King James Version,* public domain.

The image used on the cover was taken by the author during the 2024 eclipse.

Published by:

Kingdom Come Books
18896 Greenwell Springs Road
Greenwell Springs, LA 70739

www.thepublishedword.com

ISBN: 978-1-964665-01-6

Printed in the U.S., the U.K. and Australia
For Worldwide Distribution

Dedication

This book is dedicated to my wife, Lady Mary A. Washington, who has dedicated her life in ministry to serving children and families in need. Mary has stood in the courtrooms of justice and petitioned judges to provide better paths for children in abusive home situations. She has volunteered to work with the local advocacy program in our area and started the Heaven's Helping Hands Outreach Ministry. Mary is always looking to help someone. God bless you and continue the great work you do for others.

The Call to Salvation

Please read the scriptures below to be saved by the grace of God. If you confess with your mouth the Lord Jesus and believe in your heart that God has raised Him from the dead, you are saved:

Romans 10:1

Brethren, my hearts desire and prayer to God for Israel is that they might be saved

Romans 10:8

But what saith it? The word is nigh thee, even in thy mouth, and in thy heart: the word of faith, which we preach.

Romans 10:9

That if thou shalt confess with thy mouth the Lord Jesus, and shalt believe in thine heart that God has raised him from the dead, thou shalt be saved.

Welcome to the Body of Christ!

Please join a Bible-believing, Bible-teaching ministry in your area to continue your growth in God's Word.

You can also join our online ministry. For the ministry schedule, visit:

www.kingdomkonnectionministries.com

Contents

Foreword by Dr. Charles H. Washington

I am Dr. Charles H. Washington, DBA, a retired Marine Corps Master Gunnery Sergeant, small business owner and author of the book entitled *The Passion of Barbering: A New Era of Hair Designer.*[1] More importantly, I am Bishop Rodrick Leroy Washington's only living paternal uncle.

I remember the day Rodrick was brought home from the hospital. As the Washington and Beverly family gathered to welcome our newest Washington to the clan, it was noticed that the matriarch of the family, his grandmother Nezie, appeared to make a uniquely godly bond with the infant.

When Rodrick was born, I was in high school. Until I finished high school and joined the

---

1. Bloomington, Indiana (iUniverse Publishing:2015)

military, I watched his growth from infancy through kindergarten. I noticed that he was always fascinated with books, even if he had no idea what was in those books. This came from watching his grandmother Nezie reading the Bible.

Even as a small boy, Rodrick enjoyed visiting with his grandma, who was frequently referred to as "Mother Dear." She was always taking him shopping, cooking something he liked, or taking him to church with her.

After graduating high school, Rodrick joined the military and upon fulfilling his obligation and being discharged, he returned to his roots in Mobile, Alabama. It was there where he first realized that his goal in life was to bring men closer to Christ. For more than twenty-eight years, Grandma Nezie was President of the Pastor's Aid Board for Mount Olive Baptist Church #1, located at 409 Lexington Avenue in Mobile, Alabama. Once Rodrick was ordained, Grandma Nezie nurtured and guided him through the network and getting known by the local clergy members.

The title of the book, *Where Will I Spend Eternity?* is a not-so-simple question we must all

Bishop R. L. Washington Sr.

consider, and godly manifested principles are a road map one should embrace. I am writing this forward and endorsing this book because I have seen firsthand through Bishop Washington's life how biblically sound principles in concert with the Bible will manifest joy and comfort in your life.

Charles H. Washington

Foreword by Stephanie Bernard

I came to know and was introduced to Bishop R.L. Washington Sr. by my oldest sister, Mary Jane Brookins, in 1997. She joined the ministry, along with her husband, Adolph Brookins Sr., who served as Bishop's Armor Bearer.

Mrs. Brookins, as Bishop called her, was Chief Administrator for the Lake Jackson Worship Center and Kingdom Konnection Ministries under Bishop's pastoral leadership. Mrs. Brookins and Bishop were spiritual acquaintances and very close friends until her untimely death in 2021.

In July of 2007, Bishop started the Kingdom Konnection Prayer line, where he taught the Word of God every week to hearers across the country via teleconference. During the COVID 19 Pandemic in 2020, when churches were closed, Bishop moved KKM online to continue outreach to followers across the country.

Where Will I Spend Eternity?

Bishop has superior knowledge, understanding, and wisdom to expound on the Word of God, and many have become affiliated with his ministry because of his ability to make the Word of God plain, with simplicity and understanding.

Personally, my spiritual knowledge has expanded beyond my expectations from hearing the Word taught with simplicity to the understanding level of a child. The teachings are intense, repetitious, and powerful to the Spirit man. From a young girl, I had attended church but had never heard the Word of God taught with such impact and passion.

Of all the teachings that I've had the privilege to hear Bishop teach, the message of *Where Will I Spend Eternity?* has been the deepest and most captivating of them all.

I had been taught over the years that if we died in Christ, we would go to Heaven to live with God, but Revelation 21:3 states:

> *And I heard a great voice out of heaven saying, Behold, the tabernacle of God is with*

Bishop R. L. Washington Sr.

men, and he will dwell with them, and they shall be his people, and God himself shall be with them, and be their God.

Therefore, we are not going up to live with Him; He is coming to dwell with us!

It is imperative for readers to know the truth about where we're going after death. The answer to that age-old question: *Where Will I Spend Eternity?* will be found in the reading of this book.

Minister Stephanie Bernard

And I heard a great voice out of heaven saying, Behold, the tabernacle of God is with men, and he will dwell with them, and they shall be his people, and God himself shall be with them, and be their God.

–Revelation 21:3

Author's Preface

After thirty years in ministry, I never thought writing a book about eternity or end times would be so beneficial to the Body of Christ. Over the years, hearing parishioners say "Heaven is our home" or "to be absent from the body, is to be present with the Lord" never resonated with me. So, I studied this subject for more than five years and decided to teach it. Then, I was encouraged by my students to write a book on *Where Will I Spend Eternity?*

Bishop R.L. Washington, Sr
Presiding Prelate, KKM

Part 1

The Outline of the Book

THE NAME: The English word *revelation* was derived from the original Greek word *apocalypse,* which means "to uncover or reveal." This is the revelation given to John, disciple of Jesus.

The book of Revelation can be broken down into seven ages or eras for our consideration and in-depth study.

1. The Manifestation Era (Chapter 1)
   The Vision God Revealed to John

2. The Congregation Era (Chapters 2 and 3)
   The Church Age

3. The Celebration Era (Chapters 4, 5, and 19)
   The Rapture of the Church

Where Will I Spend Eternity?

4. The Tribulation Era (Chapters 6 through 18)
   The Tribulation of the Unrighteous

5. The Condemnation Era (Chapter 20)
   The Judgement Seat of Christ

6. The Restoration Era (Chapter 21)
   The New Jerusalem

7. The Consecration Era (Chapter 22)
   Eternal Life

Part 2

An Introduction to Revelation

And I heard a great voice out of heaven say-
ing, Behold, the tabernacle of God is with
men, and he will dwell with them, and they
shall be his people, and God himself shall be
with them, and be their God.

Revelation 21:3

Preserving (preservation) our place in the New Jerusalem can only be done by reserving (reservation) our place in the New Jerusalem. This can only be done by accepting Jesus Christ as Lord and Savior (see Romans 10:9).

What are we saved from? I'm glad you asked!
- We are saved from satanic influence (see Luke 22:31).
- We are saved from self-inflicted wounds (see Romans 7:18-20).

Where Will I Spend Eternity?

- We are saved from a sinful environment (see Romans 7:12-13 and 6:12).

Romans 6:23 declares, *"The wages of sin is death."* Therefore salvation guarantees everlasting life with God in eternity (see John 3:16).

- We are saved for the Rapture (see 1 Thessalonians 5:13-17)

- We are saved from the seven-year tribulation (see Revelation 6-18).

- We are saved for the thousand-year millennial reign with Christ (see Revelation 20:1-4).

- We are saved from the final judgement (see Revelation 20:11-15).

Part 3

Revelation 1:9

I John, ... was in the isle that is called Patmos.

The Isle of Patmos is not an island at all; it's a small strip of land located off the west coast of Turkey, today belonging to Greece.

Patmos is only seven and a half miles in length and six miles in width. John was exiled there to die after surviving being dropped into hot grease and not losing a single piece of flesh from his body.

Patmos was:

- Unoccupied (no one lived there)
- Uncivilized (wild animals and beasts roamed the isle)
- Unidentified (not recognized as anything of value)

Where Will I Spend Eternity?

Because John was taken there, he understood three things about his journey:

- THE PURPOSE–John was there for the Word (voice) and the witness (vision) of Jesus Christ.

- THE PLACE–It was called Patmos, meaning "my killing."

- THE PLAN–He was sent there to die.

Revelation 1:1a – The Messiah (Savior)

Revelation 1:1b – The Messenger (Sacred)

Revelation 1:2 – The Message (Sovereign)

Part 4

Revelation 1:10-13

VERSE 10 — *"I was in the Spirit."* How to get in the Spirit (see Acts 10:10, Galatians 5:16-23, and 1 Corinthians 6:9-12).

On the Savior's day, John heard a sound, *"a great voice, as of a trumpet."*

Concerning the place called *"Patmos"*:

VERSE 11 — The Savior was there on the isle.

VERSE 12 — The seven golden candlesticks mentioned in verse 12 were the seven church in Asia Minor.

VERSE 11 — The Voice (The Christ)
VERSE 12 — The Vision (The Churches)
VERSE 13 — The Victory (The Chosen One)

Where Will I Spend Eternity?

Two things were done with the message of John's revelation to get the Word to the churches:

1. IT WAS TRANSPORTED (transportation): The message was "moved" from the heart of God to Jesus, to the angel, to John (see Revelation 1:1), to the churches.

2. IT WAS TRANSPLANTED: *Transplant* is a surgical procedure in which organs or tissue are moved from one body to another to prolong life. In the midst of John's apocalypse (revelation), he found himself *"in the Spirit,"* which is a great place to be.

Part 5

Revelation 1
The Vision

John the Revelator was on the Isle of Patmos, located in Asia Minor. He was exiled there to die, left without food or other provisions and with wild animals roaming the area, seeking their next prey.

Patmos was in the Aegean Sea west of Greece and east of Turkey, only accessible by boat.

VERSE 1—Jesus Christ sent a message to John for His servants by His angel (THE MESSIAH).

VERSE 2—*"The testimony of Jesus Christ"* (THE MESSENGER)

VERSE 3—To read or hear this prophecy is a blessing. *"The time is at hand."* (THE MESSAGE)

VERSE 4—"The seven spirits" (THE MEMBERSHIP)

VERSE 11—*"Write what thou seest in a book and send it unto the seven churches which are in Asia."* (THE ASSIGNMENT)

VERSE 12—The seven candlesticks (churches) of Revelation 1:20 were listening. (THE AUDIENCE)

VERSE 13—Jesus was standing *"in the midst of"* the seven churches (see Revelation 2 and 3).

VERSES 14-16—A description of Jesus, our Savior (ALPHA AND OMEGA)

(See Daniel 10:5-6) Daniel chapters 6 through 10 contain a vision of promise of the Savior. Daniel described Jesus in the lion's den just as John did, but thousands of years before (see also Ezekiel's vision, Ezekiel 43).

VERSE 17— *"FEAR NOT!"* 2 Timothy 1:7 *"For God hath not given us a spirit of fear."*

Bishop R. L. Washington Sr.

VERSE 18—Compare with 8. *"Which is"* (*"he that liveth*), *"which was"* (here on earth), *"which is to come"* (the return of the Messiah).

Part 6

Revelation 2
The Congregation Era

The personalities of the seven churches in Asia Minor:

- The Church at Ephesus was selfish (see Revelation 2:1-7, especially verse 4).

- The Church at Smyrna was suffering (see Revelation 2:8-11, especially verses 9 and 10)

- The Church at Pergamos was satanic (see Revelation 2:12-17, especially verse 13).

- The Church at Thyatira was struggling (see Revelation 2:18-29, especially verse 20).

Bishop R. L. Washington Sr.

- The Church at Sardis was sleepy
  (see Revelation 3:1-6, especially verse 3).

- The Church at Philadelphia was steady
  (see Revelation 3:7-13, especially verse 8).

- The Church at Laodicea was stubborn
  (see Revelation 3:14-22, especially verse 16).

Jesus gives a threefold message here for each of the churches:

SALUTATION — He introduces Himself to each church.

INSPIRATION–He gives a message of hope to each church.

DEVASTATION–He provides clear direction on how each church needs to improve to remain in fellowship with Him.

Revelation 2:1-7
The Church at Ephesus

The Church at Ephesus was an ancient, historical church located in Asia Minor.

HER SALUTATION–Revelation 2:1

HER INSPIRATION–Revelation 2:2-3

HER DEVASTATION–Revelation 2:4-5

Revelation 2:8-11
The Church at Smyrna

The Church at Smyrna was a factory, working-class church.

HER SALUTATION — Revelation 2:8

HER INSPIRATION–Revelation 2:9-10 (see also 2 Corinthians 8:9)

HER DEVASTATION — Revelation 2:9-10 (see also Matthew 15:8, 1 Timothy 6:7-9 and 17-19).

Part 9

Revelation 2:12-17
The Church at Pergamos

The Church at Pergamos was at a tourist attraction, a place where people went to enjoy themselves.

HER SALUTATION–Revelation 2:12

HER INSPIRATION–Revelation 2:13

HER DEVASTATION—Revelation 2:14

Balak, King of the Moabites and Balaam (vs 14) cursed the children of Israel.

Antipas (vs 13), one of the saints at Pergamos was a disciple of John.

Part 10

Revelation 2:18-28
The Church at Thyatira

The Church at Thyatira was apostolic and very religious.

HER SALUTATION — Revelation 2:18

HER INSPIRATION — Revelation 2:19

HER DEVASTATION — Revelation 2:20

Jezebel was scheming, evil, shameless, and wicked. She was not a spirit but a personality, the pagan wife of King Ahab.

How do we overcome the Jezebel personality?

- RECOGNITION — Verse 22
- REPENTANCE — Verse 22
- RECEPTION — Verses 26-27

Part 11

Revelation 3:1-6
The Church at Sardis

The Church at Sardis was very wealthy.

HER SALUTATION—Revelation 3:1 (See also Romans 8:6-8. Flesh will never please God.)

HER INSPIRATION—Revelation 3:2

HER DEVASTATION—Revelation 3:1C *"[thou] art dead"* (remembrance, receptance, and repentance).

Part 12

Revelation 3:7-13
The Church at Philadelphia

The Church at Philadelphia was loving and kind. However, their environment was corrupt.

HER SALUTATION – Revelation 3:7 (See also John 21:15. Three types of love: *agape, phileo,* and *storge*)

HER INSPIRATION – Revelation 3:7 (Revelation 3:9 says they were counterfeit Jews.)

HER DEVASTATION – Revelation 3:8 (In verse 10, there was *"temptation,"* and the people had to choose between fidelity and infidelity).

Where Will I Spend Eternity?

Jesus was tempted in three common areas:

1. Hedonism, the lust of the body (hunger)
2. Egoism, the pride of life (strength)
3. Materialism, the lust of the eyes (wealth)

Part 13

Revelation 3:14-22
The Church at Laodicea

The Church at Laodicea was a community church in Asia Minor.

HER SALUTATION–Revelation 3:14

HER INSPIRATION–This church received no inspiration from God as they were straddling the fence and needed to choose righteousness over selfishness.

HER DEVASTATION–Revelation 3:15-17

VERSE 15—This church was on the fence.

VERSE 16—They were rejected by God. *"I will spue thee out of my mouth."*

VERSES 17-18—Offered restoration *"buy of me"* (see also Luke 6:38 and Malachi 3:10).

VERSE 19—Repentance

Part 14

The Rapture

The Rapture (being caught up) will take place immediately after the Church Era of Revelation 2 and 3.

For the end times, see Matthew 24:3-6, 14 and 29-30.

The Rapture was described by Paul in 1 Thessalonians 4:13-17:

Verse 13—**DEVASTATION**, hopelessness

Verse 14—CONFIRMATION, hope in Jesus

Verse 15—IMPARTATION, *"by the word of the Lord."*

Verse 16—RESURRECTION, *"The dead in Christ shall rise."*

Where Will I Spend Eternity?

Verse 17—CONSECRATION, being set apart as the Body of Christ

Part 15

The Resurrected Body

1 Corinthians 15:35 — *"What body?"*

1 John 3:2 — A body like Jesus'

Luke 24:36-39 — A physical body

John 20:26 — Thomas' contact with the physical body of Jesus, unlimited by nature

1 Corinthians 15:40-44 — Glorified bodies

Luke 16:19-31 — The rich man and Lazarus

Luke 23:43 — *"Today shalt thou be with me in paradise."*

Where Will I Spend Eternity?

1 Peter 3:18-20—*"Preached unto the spirits in prison"* (vs 19).

Part 16

Revelation 4
The Invitation, the Twenty-Four Elders and the Four Beasts

VERSE 1—The Invitation, *"Come up hither."*

Revelation 1:19 gives us insight into the three dimensions:

- *"Which thou hast seen"* – past
- *"Which are"* – present
- *"Which shall be hereafter"* – future

VERSE 4—The Twenty-Four Elders.
They are separated into two parts: twelve from the tribes of Israel, representing the Old Testament, and the twelve apostles, representing the New Testament.

Where Will I Spend Eternity?

VERSE 7—The Four Beasts

- The Lion–Wild, untamed animals
- The Calf—Domesticated, tamed animals
- The Man–Humanity
- The Eagle–King, representing the fowls of the air

In Genesis 1:28, God gave man dominion over all of His creation. (For a complete understanding, read the complete chapter.)

Part 17

Revelation 4
The Throne of God

VERSE 1 — What's heard from the throne?

VERSES 2-3 — Who's on the throne?

VERSE 4 — Who's around the throne?

VERSE 5a — What's coming from the throne?

VERSE 5b — What's burning before the throne?

VERSE 6a — What lies before the throne?

VERSE 6b — What's round about the throne?

All things are created *"for thy pleasure"* Revelation 4:11 (See also Genesis 1:31).

Part 18

Revelation 5

Verses 1-4—The transition into the tribulation. The angel is saddened after finding no one to open the book and loose the seals of wrath.

Verses 5-6—The Lamb in the midst of the elders who were slain

Verses 7-8—The call to worship after the Lamb receives the book

Verses 9-10—*"Redeemed to God"* by the blood of the Lamb

Verses 11-14—The worship in Heaven begins.

Next up, the seven-year tribulation period.

Part 19

The Tribulation

The tribulation (or troubled) era will last seven years.

Revelation 11:2 — 42 months = 3 ½ years
Revelation 11:3 — 1,260 days = 3 ½ years

The tribulation era will have twenty-one "wraths" unleashed on those with the mark of the beast who did not accept Christ as Savior and Lord during the congregational or church era (see Romans 10:9). This period will witness:

- The opening of the seven seals, Revelation 6:1 (seal #1) through Revelation 8:1 (seal #7)

- The sounding of the seven trumpets (see Revelation 8:2)

- The pouring out of the seven vials of wrath (see Revelation 16)

The Lamb of God will open all seven seals while angels sound trumpets and pour out their respective vials (see Revelation 5:1-6).

Part 20

Revelation 6
The First Six Vials

VERSES 1-2—Seal #1

VERSE 1—The four beasts send the invitation: *"Come and see"*

VERSE 2—The white horse symbolizes a fight, *"Conquering and to conquer."* (See also Zechariah 6:1-8, a vision of the fours spirits.)

Verses 3-4—Seal #2. In verse 4, the red horse symbolizes fear, taking peace from the earth.

VERSES 5-6—Seal #3. The black horse of verse 5 symbolizes famine. (Verse 6: *"See thou hurt not the oil and the wine."*)

VERSES 7-8—Seal #4. The pale horse of verse 8 symbolizes death, *"and hell followed with him."*

Where Will I Spend Eternity?

Verses 9-11—Seal #5. The souls under the altar were *"slain for the word of God."*

Verse 12—Seal #6. The crumbling of the Universe. (See also Joel 2:10, his prophecy of the Day of the Lord.)

Verse 13—Celestial destructiveness

Verse 14—Heavenly chaos

Verse 15—Kings, slaves, and mighty men alike hide themselves.

Verses 16-17—They are hiding from the mighty hand of the Lamb of God.

Part 21

Revelation 7

Verses 1-3—Preparation to seal the 144,000

Verse 4—The 144,000, made up of the twelve tribes of Israel, are sealed.

Verse 5—Juda, Reuben, and Gad, 12,000 each tribe = 36,000.

Verse 6—Aser, Nepthalim, and Manasses, 12,000 each tribe = 36,000.

Verse 7—Simeon, Levi, and Issachar, 12,000 each tribe = 36,000.

Verse 8—Zabulon, Joseph, and Benjamin, 12,000 each tribe =36,000.

Where Will I Spend Eternity?

Verse 9 — A great multitude of white-robed servants (see Revelation 6:9-11) will be slain for the Word of God.

Verse 14 — These white-robed servants have come *"out of great tribulation, and have washed their robes, and made them white in the blood of the Lamb."*

Part 22

Revelation 8
The Final Seal

VERSE 1 — The seventh and final seal (silence in Heaven for half an hour). What started with thunder (problems, see Revelation 6:1) ends with silence (peace, see Revelation 8:1).

VERSE 2 — The angels prepare to sound the seven trumpets assigned to them.

VERSE 2 — The angels are given the seven trumpets (reception).

VERSE 6 — The angels are prepared to sound (preparation).

VERSE 7 — The first angel sounds (an atmospheric attack). The lowest layer of the atmosphere starts at ground level up to 6.2 miles or 33,000 feet.

Where Will I Spend Eternity?

VERSES 8-9—The second angel sounds (a stratospheric attack). The second layer of the atmosphere begins from four to twelve miles above the Earth.

VERSE 10—The third angel sounds (a mesospheric attack). The third layer of the atmosphere, air too thin to breathe, begins at fifty miles above the Earth, extending above the stratosphere.

VERSE 11—*Wormwood* means "bitter or poisonous."

VERSE 12—The fourth angel sounds (a thermospheric attack). The fourth layer of the atmosphere starts at fifty miles to four hundred and forty miles above the Earth.

Of the seven atmospheric layers, four of them are used in this chapter. (There is more to come on these very powerful attacks that will be launched against the enemy.)

Part 23

Revelation 9:1-12
The Fifth Angel Sounds

VERSES 1-3—As the fifth angel sounds, there is an exospheric attack, only observable from space. The exosphere is at least sixty thousand miles above the surface of the Earth

VERSE 1—Matthew 16:14-19 speaks of the keys to the Kingdom. Here a key is given to an angel to control entry and exit

VERSE 2—The bottomless pit. Locusts are given the power of scorpions. (See Joel 2 for his prophecy of the last days of damnation).

VERSE 3—Locusts are given control.

VERSE 4—Locusts are given a command.

Where Will I Spend Eternity?

VERSE 5—Locusts conquer man for five months.

VERSE 11—Both the Greek word for *Apollyon* and the Hebrew word for *Abaddon* mean "destroyer."

The Bottomless Pit is a deep chasm in the heart of the Earth otherwise known as Hell or Sheol.

Part 24

Revelation 9:13-21
The Sixth Angel Sounds

VERSE 13—A voice is heard. According to Exodus 30:1-3, an altar is a holy place, not for sinners (see also John 9:31).

VERSE 14—The *Euphrates,* meaning "to gush or break out" (see Genesis 2:10-14), is a river in western Asia, the longest part of which flows through Syria and Iraq and empties into the Persian Gulf.

VERSE 15—Four angels execute a third of the existing population of the Earth.

VERSE 16—The mounted horsemen number 200 million

VERSE 17-18—The heads of the horses were of lions. Four dominions of God (see Revelation 4:7, the lion, the calf, the man, and the flying eagle).

VERSE 19-21—They have power in their tails (see Isaiah 9:15). The devil is the tail.

Part 25

Revelation 10

VERSE 1—The power of nature covers the mighty angel, meaning that he has power over all nature: *"a cloud," "a rainbow," "the sun,"* and *"fire."*

VERSE 2—The *"little book"* represents prophecy, meaning the Word of God through prophecy (see verse 11 and Matthew 28:18).

VERSES 3-4–The seven thunders (seals). God will reveal what was uttered through vision. (See also Daniel 8:26 and Revelation 10:7, the mystery of God, the 144,000).

VERSES 5-6—The angel took an oath before the throne of God and swore that time had run out and the plan of God through tribulation would continue.

VERSE 8—John takes the book, the transfer of power from the angel to himself.

VERSE 9—In his belly it is bitter, although in his mouth it is sweet (see also Jeremiah 15:16, *"Thy words were found, and I did eat them."*

VERSE 10—John eats the book.

VERSE 11—We *"must"* preach the Word of God to all nations, peoples and tongues.

Part 26

Revelation 11:1-14

Israel is still in unbelief at this point of the tribulation. The Temple will eventually be destroyed by the Antichrist.

VERSE 1—These events will happen in the city where Jesus was crucified (see verse 8). Measurements represent the spiritual condition of the Jews.

VERSE 2—Israel and the Holy City will be oppressed by Gentiles and suffer for forty-two months (see Luke 21:21-24, Jesus' prophecy to the disciples).

VERSE 3—The two witnesses will prophesy for 1,260 days or three and a half years.

Verses 4-5—The two witnesses will be protected from harm in the presence of God.

Where Will I Spend Eternity?

VERSE 6—The ministry of each witness will identify who he is:

- Elijah shut up the heavens with his prophecy of no rain (see 1 Kings 17:1). He did not see death (see 2 Kings 2:11).
- Moses had power over water to turn it to blood (see Exodus 7:20). He died and was buried (see Deuteronomy 34:5-6).
- Enoch (see Genesis 5:21-24) is not one of the two witnesses.

VERSE 7—Both witnesses will die, and their bodies will lie in the streets in the same city where Jesus was crucified (again see verse 8).

Part 27

Revelation 11:15-19

The Seventh Angel Sounds

Verse 15—Heaven announces the Kingdom takeover, and Christ will reign forever (see also 2 Corinthians 4:3-4).

Verse 16—The twenty-four elders engage in worship (that's adoration). In verses 16 and 17, they fall upon their faces, giving God thanks.

Verse 17—The twenty-four elders engage in word (that's impartation). *"Which art"* (present), *"and wast"* (past) and *"art to come"* (future).

Verse 18—The twenty-four elders engage in wrath (that's correction). Nations are angry, wrath will come, and the dead shall be judged.

Verse 18—The twenty-four elders engage in witness (that's redemption). Reward is for *"the prophets," "the saints,"* and *"all them that fear [God's] name."*

Verse 18—The twenty-four elders engage in waste (that's destruction). They will destroy those who destroy the earth.

Verse 19— The Temple (see 1 Corinthians 6:19-20)

Part 28

Revelation 12:1-6

VERSE 1—A woman (Israel) is *"clothed with the sun"* and standing on the moon. The *"twelve stars"* represent the twelve tribes of Israel—Old Testament.

VERSE 2—She is pregnant with the promise to the world—Jesus, born of the Old Testament tribe of Judah. Verse 5 describes His role and will reveal His identity.

VERSES 3-4— *"Seven heads and ten horns"* plus *"seven crowns"* = the twenty-four elders. These represent the Old Testament and the New Testament coming together. The dragon seeking to kill the king at birth represents King Herod of the New Testament.

VERSE 6 — The woman (Israel) flees to the wilderness for protection for three and a half years of the tribulation. In Revelation 11:3, the two witnesses prophesy for the exact same amount of time.

- The horn is a symbol of strength (see Daniel 7).
- The head is a sign of power.
- The crown is a symbol of kingship.

Part 29

Revelation 12:7-14

VERSES 7-9—*"War in heaven,"* EXPULSION (see also Ezekiel 28:7-10 and Isaiah 14:12).

VERSE 10—CELEBRATION because of Satan's departure (see also Isaiah 44:23 and 49:13).

VERSE 11—Satan is overcome by the blood of the Lamb and the word of their testimony, RESTORATION.

VERSE 12— PREPARATION for war on the earth

VERSE 13—PERSECUTION

Verse 14—PROTECTION

Part 30

Revelation 13:1-8

Verse 1—The ten horns are the ten kingdoms (see Revelation 17:12).

Compare Daniel:
- Daniel 7:24-28— Daniels vision of Revelation 13:1
- Daniel 2:44— God's Kingdom
- Daniel 7:7—The beast vision from Daniel

Compare also Revelation 17:9:
> The seven heads (or kings) and *"seven mountains in which the woman sitteth."*

VERSE 2—Compare Daniel 7:3-6 contains Daniel's vision of the beast. Daniel 8:23-25 describes the Old Roman Empire.

VERSE 3—*"Wounded to death"* It appears to the whole earth that the Antichrist has suffered a fatal wound but is brought back to life again by the supernatural power of Satan (see also 2 Thessalonians 2:9-10). Satan's supernatural power will deceive many (see Revelation 13:14 and 2 Thessalonians 2:9-12).

VERSES 4-5—The enemy has forty-two months to deceive during the last half of the tribulation period of seven years. *"Speaking blasphemies."*

VERSE 6— *"Blasphemy against God"*

VERSE 7— *"War with the saints"*

VERSE 8—The unsaved worship the Antichrist.

Part 31

Revelation 13:11-15

VERSE 11 — The beast of the earth will help the beast from the sea (see verse 12). Two horns – deception to portray itself as an humble, gentle, loving, kind personality (*"like a lamb,"* NOT *as* a lamb. However, his character is *"as a dragon"* (see also Matthew 7:5).

Verse 12 — A deadly wound is healed before all to lead those on earth to worship the first beast. This will be the start of the false church that worships the Antichrist.

VERSES 13-14 — Idolatry (idol worship). God warns against this in Deuteronomy 13:1-3 in reference to the children of Israel. The ministry of the Antichrist will be counterfeit, mimicking the works of the Holy Spirit.

Bishop R. L. Washington Sr.

VERSE 15—A decree will be given to kill those who will not worship the image of the beast. In Revelation 6:9, John saw the martyred souls under the altar (see Revelation 14:12-13).

Part 32

Revelation 13:16-18
666

VERSE 16—Satan will take total control of the world's financial system. The mark in the right hand or forehead is key, suggesting the possibility of implanted chips to track people and control the global economy.

2 Corinthians 4:4 declares that Satan is *"the god of this world,"* and this economic takeover will prove that. Remember, we, the people of God, are not *of* this world. We are just *in* this world temporarily.

VERSE 18—Six is the number of man and denotes weakness and satanic influence. 666 is the number of the Beast and denotes evil.

Bishop R. L. Washington Sr.

- Man was created on the sixth day (see Genesis 1:26-312).

- Man would serve six years and in the seventh year be free, the year of Jubilee (see Exodus 21:2).

- Jesus hung on the cross in darkness from the sixth to the ninth hour (see Luke 23:44 and Matthew 27:45).

- Jephthah served six years as judge over Israel. He was born in Gilead and his mother was a prostitute. His family drove him out of power because he was considered illegitimate. He then moved to live among scoundrels (see Judges 11 and 12).

- There were six earthquakes listed in the Bible (see Exodus 19:16-18, 1 Kings 19:11, Amos 1:1-2, Matthew 27:50-51, 28:2, and Acts 16:25-26).

- Jesus was accused of being demon possessed six times (see Mark 3:22, John 7:20,

Where Will I Spend Eternity?

8:48, 8:52, 10:20 and Luke 11:15).

- There are six Bible references to people practicing witchcraft or sorcery (see Matthew 24:24, Acts 13:4-52, 14:1-25, Acts 16:16, 19:13, and 19:14-16).

- Here are six references where Jesus was asked to prove that He was God (Matthew 12:38, Mark 8:11, Matthew 16:1, Matthew 24:3, Mark 13:4], Luke 11:16 and John 2:18).

Part 33

Revelation 14:1-5
The Inauguration of the Kingdom of God on Earth

VERSE 1—Demarcation, boundaries, set limits (see Revelation 7:1-8).

VERSE 2—Consecration (the voice of God leading worship).

VERSE 3—Redemption (bought with the blood and engaging in worship).

VERSES 4-5—Reconciliation

Part 34

Revelation 14:6-20

VERSE 6—The angelic hosts proclaim the Gospel to the world as the seven-year tribulation comes to an end.

VERSE 7—The first angel declares, *"The hour of his judgement is come."*

VERSE 8—The second angel declares, *"Babylon is fallen."* Babylon, in Hebrew, means "gate of God." It was derived from the root word *babel*, which means "to jumble or confuse." This represents the time between the rebuilding of Jerusalem and the coming of Jesus Christ.

Three world systems will fall and ultimately fail:

Bishop R. L. Washington Sr.

- THE COMMERCIAL SYSTEM— Buying and selling, commerce
- THE POLITICAL SYSTEM–Kings and other leaders are dethroned.
- THE ECCLESIASTICAL SYSTEM– The religious community is persecuted. Revelation 18 and 19 will provide more detail.

The Babylonian captivity under Nebuchadnezzar (see Daniel 9:24) lasted for seventy weeks, each week representing seven years, for a total of four hundred and ninety years. Babylon became a symbol of evil.

VERSES 9-14—The third angel declares, *"If any man worship the beast ... ."*

VERSES 15-16—The fourth angel declares, *"The time is come for thee to reap."*

VERSE 17—The fifth angel has a sharp sickle in his hand.

VERSE 18—The sixth angel is commanded to attack.

VERSE 19—"The winepress of the wrath of God" (see also Isaiah 63:3-4, Revelation 19:15-20, Matthew 25:32 and Psalm 110.

Part 35

Revelation 15

Heaven prepares to release the final judgement of doom on the earth to end the tribulation. God takes complete control over the enemy.

VERSE 1—*"Seven angels having the seven last plagues"* of doom.

VERSE 2—These are the souls who made it out of the tribulation and did not bow to the beast.

VERSES 3-4—They are singing their testimony of praise to God.

VERSE 5—The temple (se Exodus 32:15 and 40:34-38)

Verse 6-8—The order for God's wrath to be released

Part 36

Revelation 16

VERSE 1—Seven angels prepare to pour out the final seven vials of wrath upon the earth (see also Daniel 11:36-45).

VERSE 2—THE FIRST VIAL—Sores (see also Exodus 9:8, the plague of boils).

VERSE 3—The SECOND VIAL—The sea becomes blood (see also Exodus 7:14).

VERSE 4—THE THIRD VIAL—The rivers and fountains become blood (see also Exodus 7:20-25).

VERSE 8—THE FOURTH VIAL—A scorching sun (see also 2 Corinthians 4:1-4 and Deuteronomy 32:5).

Verse 10—THE FIFTH VIAL—Darkness (see also Exodus 10:21).

Verse 12—THE SIXTH VIAL—The River Euphrates is dried up.

Verse 13—Unclean spirits are released. The dragon, the beast, and false prophet (the beast of sea and the beast of the earth).

Verses 17-20—THE SEVENTH VIAL—An earthquake *"such as was not since men were upon the earth."*

Part 37

Revelation 17

VERSE 5 — *"Mystery, Babylon the Great"* Jeremiah's prophecy concerning the fall of Babylon played an important part in the history of redemption (see Jeremiah 50:1). The people of God were in exile at the time of these events, and the danger of being assimilated into a new culture was imminent. Babylon, located south of Baghdad in Iraq, was rich in commerce and art.

Spiritual Babylon is divided into three components:

POLITICALLY: the Babylonian Empire will be destroyed by Christ at His second coming (see Revelation 19:11-21).

Bishop R. L. Washington Sr.

RELIGIOUSLY: The Great Whore will be destroyed by the Antichrist (see verses 16-17, Isaiah 1:21, Jeremiah 3:9 and 2:26-27).

COMMERCIALLY: Money systems will be destroyed by the mark of the beast (see Revelation 13:16-18).

Part 38

Revelation 18

VERSES 1-3—*"Babylon the great is fallen!"* This is not the city of Babylon, but the spirit of Babylon.

In 586 BC, Babylon invaded Judah and destroyed Jerusalem, and the Jewish people were exiled. Second Kings chapters 17 through 25 provide more detailed insight into the invasion of the Holy City of Jerusalem. Now Babylon is a symbol of sin and rebellion (see Jeremiah 21:4-10).

VERSES 4-8—The final call prior to destruction

VERSE 4—REPENTANCE

VERSE 5—RECONCILIATION

Bishop R. L. Washington Sr.

VERSE 6—REWARD

VERSE 7—The release of doom on the way

VERSES 9-11—Mourning the destruction of the spirit of Babylon

VERSES 12-16—The merchandise of that spirit is destroyed.

VERSE 17—*"In one hour,"* Babylon is doomed.

VERSES 20-24—Heaven rejoices.

VERSES 18-19—Continued mourning for the loss of Babylon

Part 39

Revelation 19:1-10
Celebration in Heaven

VERSE 1—*"Alleluia,"* a Hebrew word meaning "praise the Lord." It is made up of *halal* (praise) and *Jah* (a shortened form of Yahweh, a Hebrew word for "Lord." Heaven is a dwelling, home, or residence (see 2 Corinthians 12:2-4, Paradise, the garden of God).

John and three other voices are heard:

VERSE 1—The people's voice

VERSE 4—The patriots' voice

VERSES 5-6—A powerful voice

VERSES 7-10—*"The Lamb"* (Jesus) and *"his wife"* (the Church)

VERSE 8—She is a church without spot or wrinkle (THE CLEANSING)

VERSE 9— *"Blessed are they which are called"* (THE CALLING).

VERSE 10— *"Worship him [the Lord]"* (THE CONSECRATION).

As noted in Revelation 1:12-17, John falls at the feet of Jesus as though dead.

Part 40

Revelation 19:11-21
Dethroning the Enemy

Dethroning the Enemy (Verse 11-13)

Verse 11 — The Second Coming of Christ begins. "Heaven opened (see also 2 Corinthians 12:2-4, 2 Thessalonians 1:7-9, Psalm 96:13 and John 5:30)

Heaven–the abode of God, also the sky perceived as a vault in which the sun, moon, stars, and planets (including Earth) are situated.

Disarming the Enemy (Verses 14-16)

Verse 14 — There are armies with him (see also Revelation 7:14)

Verse 15 — *"Smite the nations"* (see also Psalm 2:9, and Matthew 24:29-30).

Bishop R. L. Washington Sr.

Verse 16—His identity: KING OF KINGS AND LORD OF LORDS.

Destroying the Enemy (Verses 17-21)

Verse 17—*"The supper of the great God"* (the Battle of Armageddon in northern Israel).

Verse 19—*"To make war"*

Verse 20—*"Both cast alive into a lake of fire"*

Verse 21—*"The remnant were slain."*

Part 41

Revelation 20:1-10
Satan's Penalty

VERSES 1-3—Punishment and deliverance from the enemy. The destruction and imprisonment of Satan.

VERSES 4-6—Paradise and the thousand-year reign of Christ. Those who sit on thrones (see also Revelation 2:7, Ezekiel 37:11-14, and Ephesians 3:1-6).

VERSES 7-9—Pardoned. Satan is loosed from prison to deceive the nations.

VERSE 10— *"Tormented day and night for ever and ever"*

Part 42

Revelation 20:11-15
Judgment

Preparation for restoration will begin with judgement and the casting away of evil.

VERSE 11—*"A great white throne"*

VERSE 12—*"The dead, small and great, stand before God."*

Verse 13—*"They were judged every man according to their works."*

VERSE 14—"The second death." Hell: The Hebrew word translated to English as *hell* is *gehenna*, which means "darkness and unquenchable fire" (see Luke 16:19-23). The Greek word for *hell* is *hades*, which is a region for departed spirits.

Where Will I Spend Eternity?

Old Testament believers who died before the resurrection of Christ will be there awaiting judgement.

Those who perish after the cross and are saved will be held in Paradise (not Heaven).

Part 43

Revelation 21:1-4
The Restoration Era

God will restore things back to the spiritual order that existed before the fall of man. There will be three phases to this restoration:

VERSE 1—REFORMATION

Reformation will start with the redemption of holy people, and all traces of sin will be erased from the earth realm (see also Psalm 102:25-27, Isaiah 66:1, 65:17, Romans 8:18-22, 2 Peter 3:13 Haggai 2:6, and 2 Peter 3:7-12).

Verse 2–TRANSFORMATION

The New Jerusalem already exists in Heaven (see Galatians 4:26, Isaiah 2:2, and Leviticus 26:11-12). *"Thy kingdom come thy will be done"* (Luke 11:2, see also Philippians 3:17-20).

Where Will I Spend Eternity?

Which heaven are we going to, the first heaven or the new heaven? I'm glad you asked. The answer is neither. Heaven is God's home, not ours.

Verses 3-4—CONSECRATION

VERSE 3—*"The tabernacle of God is with men."* In Revelation 7:9 and 15, there are a multitude of white-robed believers in the New Jerusalem.

VERSE 4—*"Wipe away all tears"* (see also Isaiah 35:10 and 65:19).

THREE GROUPS OF BELIEVERS:
1. Old Testament believers before the cross died believing (see Genesis 15:6). They believed in the Lord and will rise at the Judgement Seat of Christ.

2. Those who have died in Christ after the cross will be raptured in the air (see Romans 10:9).

3. During the thousand-year period, there will be tribulation believers (see verse 4).

Part 44

Revelation 21:5-8

Verses 5-8 — *"Behold, I make all things new."* God's statement of faith to His believers, those who made the transition from earth to eternity.

Three Covenants of Salvation:

The Abrahamic Covenant covered those who died before the resurrection of Jesus Christ but believed in the Lord (see Genesis 15:6, Luke 16:22-26, Revelation 20:4-5, Ezekiel 37:11-14, and Hebrews 11:32-40)

The Messianic Covenant covered those who died in Jesus Christ by accepting Him as Lord and Savior (see Romans 10:1 and 8-10 and Luke 23:43).

The Prophetic Covenant covers those who refuse the mark of the beast through the tribulation (see Revelation 20:4-5 and 21:1-3).

Part 45

Revelation 21:9-14

VERSE 9—THE CHRIST. *"The Lamb's wife,"* a metaphor for the New Jerusalem

VERSE 10—THE CITY. The New Jerusalem in Spirit (Revelation 21:2)

VERSE 11—THE CLOTHES. The Church is dressed and ready.

VERSES 12-14—The city is surrounded by types and symbols:

The twelve gates are our DIRECTION.

The twelve angels are our PROTECTION.

The twelve tribes are our CONNECTION.

The twelve fountains are our CELEBRATION

The twelve apostles are our IMPARTATION.

Revelation 21:15-27

The Excitement of Moving into a New House

Verses 15-17—THE DIMENSIONS of the city

Verses 18-21—THE DESIGN of the city

Verse 22—THE DEITY of the city

Verses 23-27—THE DESCENDANTS of the city

Revelation 22:1-5

VERSE 1—*"A pure river,"* symbolizing the Holy Spirit, who produces life and power (see Revelation 7:17, 21:6, Isaiah 44:3 and John 7:37-39).

VERSE 2—*"The tree of life"* (see also Genesis 2:9, 3:22 and Ezekiel 47:12).

VERSES 3-5—God, in His wise providence and infinite wisdom, will light the city forever.

Part 48

Revelation 22:6-15

Verse 6—REVELATION (see also Revelation 1:18-19)

Verse 7—CORRECTION (see also 1 Corinthians 15:51 and Romans 13:12)

Verse 8—COMPLETION (see also Revelation 1:8-11)

Verse 9—DIRECTION

Verses 10-11—PROCLAMATION (see also 1 Corinthians 3:14-17)

Verses 12-15—RECEPTION

Part 49

Revelation 22:16-21

THE REVELATION OF JESUS CHRIST

Verse 16a—*"I Jesus"* (see also Revelation 1:1).

THE INVITATION OF JESUS CHRIST

Verse 16b—*"have sent mine angel to testify unto you these things in the churches."*

THE REPUTATION OF JESUS CHRIST

Verse 16c—*"I am the root and offspring of David, and the bright and morning star,"* his natural and spiritual lineage.

THE INSPIRATION OF JESUS CHRIST

Verse 17—(See also 2:4)

Bishop R. L. Washington Sr.
THE DELEGATION OF JESUS CHRIST

VERSES 18-20

THE BENEDICTION OF JESUS CHRIST

Verse 21—*"The grace of our Lord Jesus Christ be with you all. Amen."*

Author Contact Page

You may contact Bishop R.L. Washington Sr., President and CEO of Kingdom Konnection Ministries, directly in any of the following ways:

EMAIL: bishopofkkm@yahoo.com

www.kingdomkonnectionministries.com

www.ingramcontent.com/pod-product-compliance
Lightning Source LLC
LaVergne TN
LVHW011336080426
835513LV00006B/382

* 9 7 8 1 9 6 4 6 6 5 0 1 6 *